Original title:
What We Became

Copyright © 2024 Swan Charm
All rights reserved.

Author: Swan Charm
ISBN HARDBACK: 978-9916-79-117-2
ISBN PAPERBACK: 978-9916-79-118-9
ISBN EBOOK: 978-9916-79-119-6

New Footprints on the Sand

In the morning light, they gleam,
New footprints tell a silent dream.
They whisper tales of where we've walked,
By the waves, our hearts unlocked.

Each step we take, the sun will trace,
Moments captured in this place.
The tide rolls in, erasing lines,
Yet our memories, forever shines.

With every grain, a story spun,
Together, we are two as one.
The ocean sings, the seagulls cry,
In this world, just you and I.

As shadows stretch with evening's fall,
We leave our mark, we stand so tall.
The footprints fade, but love remains,
In every heart, its echo reigns.

So as the stars begin to glow,
We walk again, soft and slow.
Hand in hand, through shifting sand,
New footprints lead—forever planned.

The Unwritten Chapters of Us

In quiet whispers, our stories grow,
Unseen pages where secrets flow.
Hand in hand, we craft our way,
In the light of a hopeful day.

Each moment penned with laughter's grace,
In the tapestry, we find our place.
With every glance, a tale is spun,
Two hearts collide, now we are one.

Resilient Roots in Fertile Ground

From soil rich with dreams anew,
We rise like trees, we break through.
Beneath the storms, we stand so tall,
In unity, we will not fall.

Branches sway with strength and pride,
In every challenge, we abide.
Nurtured by hope, we thrive and grow,
With every season, love will flow.

Threads of Memory and Dreams

Woven gently, time's soft thread,
Tales we share of words unsaid.
In twilight's calm, we reminisce,
Each memory holds a fleeting kiss.

The dreams we weave, a radiant light,
Guiding us through the deepest night.
In the fabric of our shared embrace,
Life unfolds, a timeless grace.

In the Wake of Our Echoes

In the stillness, echoes play,
Reminders of our fleeting day.
Footsteps linger on the ground,
In every silence, love is found.

As shadows dance, we find our song,
A melody where we belong.
With every heartbeat, we explore,
The traces left forevermore.

Our Ethereal Footprints

In whispers soft the shadows dance,
Echoes trace our fleeting glance.
Each step we take, a tale we weave,
In the night, our dreams believe.

The past unfolds like morning light,
Guiding us through endless night.
With every breath, a path is laid,
In silence, memories are made.

Threads that Bind and Break

Fragile cords of fate entwine,
Binding hearts that once did shine.
Yet in the tug, the threads may fray,
Leading love to drift away.

Words once sweet, now bitter soil,
Promises that we would not spoil.
Time can weather, twist, and turn,
Leaving ashes where hearts burn.

The Twilight of Yesterday

As daylight fades, our hopes remain,
Captured in the soft refrain.
Memories painted in warm hues,
A canvas of forgotten views.

Each twilight beckons what's to come,
Whispers low, a distant drum.
Though shadows fall, they hide the gleam,
In the dusk, we dare to dream.

In the Arms of Metamorphosis

Silken wings begin to show,
A transformation soft and slow.
Within the cocoon, we dream and grow,
Emerging bright from what we know.

Each phase a story, rich and bold,
In silence, secrets still unfold.
We shed the past to rise anew,
In the arms of change, we break through.

The Bridge We Crossed

Upon the river wide we stand,
Embracing dreams hand in hand.
A step to take, a leap to trust,
Together strong, in hope we rust.

The winds of change begin to blow,
As twilight paints a golden glow.
Memories woven, hearts entwined,
In every choice, our fate defined.

The echoes of the past resound,
In whispered truths, our love is found.
Each board creaks with tales of yore,
Yet beckons softly to explore.

With every heartbeat, we move along,
To melodies of a timeless song.
Across the bridge, the future calls,
In unity, we rise, we fall.

So here we stand, our spirits free,
A journey shared, just you and me.
With every step, the dawn will break,
Together strong, our paths we'll stake.

Flames of Renewal

In darkest nights, a spark ignites,
A flicker bright, through endless fights.
From ashes cold, new life will bloom,
The fire's dance dispels the gloom.

Embers whisper secret dreams,
While hope's bright light begins to beam.
Through trials faced and burdens shared,
Awakening souls who truly dared.

Each flame a story, each flicker a chance,
To rise again in a radiant dance.
With courage drawn from deep within,
We rise anew, our journey begins.

In every heart, a furnace burns,
With lessons learned and hard-won turns.
So let the flames consume our fears,
As passion flows through joyful tears.

We greet the dawn, our spirits soar,
With hands held high, we'll seek for more.
Embracing warmth, we find our way,
In flames of renewal, we shall stay.

The Canvas of Our Lives

Each stroke of paint a moment's grace,
A palette bright with every face.
Colors blend, the old and new,
In every hue, a dream rings true.

The brush of time, both soft and bold,
In every line, a story told.
Imagined worlds of hope and fear,
In every corner, memories dear.

From shadows cast to vibrant light,
We sketch our paths with all our might.
In every swirl and gentle curve,
Life's masterpiece begins to serve.

A canvas stretched across the years,
With laughter, love, and sometimes tears.
Each moment cherished, every strife,
Together crafted, the art of life.

So let us paint with hearts aligned,
With every brush, our souls combined.
A tapestry where love survives,
Together woven—the canvas thrives.

Growing Into Shadows

As daylight fades, the shadows grow,
Along the path we came to know.
In twilight's grasp, we find our place,
Embracing change with gentle grace.

Each whispered dream, a secret shared,
In darkest nights, we're unprepared.
Yet in the depth, the heart still glows,
In every shadow, a journey shows.

The trees stand tall, their branches wide,
In quiet strength, they serve as guides.
Their leaves, like thoughts, will softly sway,
In the hush of dusk, we find our way.

The night reveals what light can't see,
In shadow's arms, we come to be.
Embracing fear, yet reaching high,
Together daring, we touch the sky.

So let us grow through every shade,
In shadows deep, our dreams are laid.
With every step, through dark we roam,
In unity, we find our home.

Pages Written in the Stars

In the quiet of the night,
Whispers echo, hearts take flight.
Dreams unfold in silver beams,
Sailing on celestial streams.

Every twinkle, a story told,
Wishes penned in marks of gold.
Galaxies dance in deep blue hues,
Reminding us of all we choose.

Time stretches like a distant hand,
Guiding us to understand.
Truths not always clear and bright,
Yet they shine, a guiding light.

Beneath the velvet, stars align,
Charting paths we call divine.
Each heartbeat writes our longing,
In the sky, we find belonging.

We are but whispers in the air,
Pages turning, everywhere.
In the vast, we find our place,
Written in the stars' embrace.

Ghosts of Transformation

In the shadows, whispers mourn,
Echoes of lives, reborn.
Flickering flames of hope ignite,
Guiding lost souls through the night.

With each passing, we embrace,
Fleeting moments leave a trace.
Ghosts our past, they gently sway,
Transforming dusk into the day.

Crumbling walls hold tales profound,
Silent screams in the underground.
Every tear, a river flows,
Carving paths where wisdom grows.

When courage mixes with the fears,
And laughter dances with the tears,
We rise up from the hollow ground,
In transformation, we are found.

In the echoes, we discover,
Shadows blend as we recover.
Through the mist, we venture forth,
To find the light we seek from birth.

Carnivals of Change

In the night, the colors glow,
Dreams parade, a vibrant show.
Voices rising, laughter spills,
With the rhythm, the heart fills.

Tents of hope in every street,
Footsteps echo, life's heartbeat.
Magic woven, threads of fate,
Unfolding at the hour late.

Juggling moments, time a breeze,
Every challenge brings new keys.
As the world spins in delight,
Dance beneath the stars so bright.

Confetti falls from skies above,
In every wonder, we find love.
Spectacles of what can be,
Life's grand tapestry to see.

With each laugh, a banner flies,
Celebrating the lows and highs.
In the carnival's embrace, we dare,
To transform every dream laid bare.

Boundless In Between

In the stillness, silence breathes,
Cradling whispers, gently weaves.
Between the moments, lives a song,
A lullaby that feels so strong.

Crossroads where the shadows dance,
Inviting us to take a chance.
Each choice unfolding, bittersweet,
Paths collide where dreams and fears meet.

Space between the tick and tock,
Holds the key, the sacred clock.
In the pauses, stories grow,
In the quiet, wisdom flows.

What lies beyond the seen and told,
Mysteries that whisper bold.
In the gaps, our courage finds,
The boundless truth within our minds.

From every moment stretched so wide,
Sprouts the magic that's inside.
In the space where silence hums,
The heart, it knows, true change comes.

The Anatomy of Our Evolution

From single cells to complex beings,
We rise, we change, with time's soft hands.
In every leap, in every breath,
We weave the tale of life that stands.

In shadows deep, our stories blend,
The whispers of ancestors call.
Through trials faced and paths we bend,
Together we rise, together we fall.

Each change a thread in nature's weave,
From earth to sky, a dance of fate.
In ancient stones, our hearts believe,
The past we honor, the dreams we create.

Embracing scars and wisdom's grace,
We find ourselves in every dawn.
In unity, our fears we face,
In love and strength, our bond goes on.

Our evolution, a canvas bright,
Painted with each moment's glow.
Together we dream of endless flight,
In the heart of change, we grow.

Rays of Dawn on a Winter's Night

Shadows linger, whispers sigh,
Gaunt branches stretch toward the sky.
Yet hope ignites through frosty air,
As dawn unfolds, a promise fair.

Golden rays on snowflakes dance,
Transforming silence into a trance.
Each glimmer bright, each glint so fine,
Awakens hearts, as dreams align.

The world, it breathes, a quiet thrill,
In winter's grasp, it finds its will.
With every hue, the day reborns,
Through whispered winds, the spirit warns.

A canvas painted with pure light,
As shadows fade, the day ignites.
Each ray a story on the ground,
In hope and warmth, our souls are found.

So let us greet the dawn with cheer,
Embrace the warmth, release the fear.
For in the chill of winter's night,
Rays of dawn bring love's true light.

Underneath the Weight of Growth

Beneath the soil, roots intertwine,
In darkness deep, they stretch and climb.
Each ounce of strain, a tale to tell,
Of hope concealed in earthen shell.

As seasons change and storm clouds loom,
In every shadow, there's room to bloom.
With silent strength, we bear the load,
In trials faced, our courage showed.

For every struggle, there lies a spark,
An inner fire igniting the dark.
Through heavy rain and sun's embrace,
We rise anew, we find our place.

In pushing through, we learn to thrive,
The weight of growth keeps dreams alive.
As branches reach for skies so vast,
We celebrate the roots that last.

Together we stand amid the strife,
Embracing scars that shape our life.
For underneath, the weight we know,
Is where the strongest flowers grow.

The Loom of Destiny

Threads of time, so deftly spun,
In the weaver's hands, our lives begun.
Colors blend in patterns bright,
Each choice a stitch in day and night.

The future calls with haunting grace,
In every twist, we find our place.
Woven dreams and fears alike,
In the loom of life, we strike.

As fate unfolds its intricate lace,
Each moment shared, a warm embrace.
In joys and sorrows, tales unwind,
Our destinies are intertwined.

With gentle hands, we shape the thread,
In love and loss, the heart is led.
Through woven paths, we seek the light,
In shadows cast, our hopes take flight.

So let us weave in colors bold,
In every story, let love be told.
For in the fabric of our dreams,
The loom of destiny brightly gleams.

The Legacy We Forge

In shadows deep, we plant our dreams,
With every step, a silent theme.
The paths we take, they intertwine,
A legacy, in heart, we sign.

Through trials faced, we rise anew,
With every breath, our spirits grew.
In kindness shared, our story glows,
The legacy of love, it flows.

We carve our names on time's expanse,
In fleeting moments, we take a chance.
For what we leave, must sparkle bright,
A beacon in the endless night.

Hand in hand, we'll face the storm,
Together, we're forever warm.
In whispered tales, we find our voice,
In unity, we make the choice.

With every laugh and every tear,
We shape our fate, we persevere.
In harmony, our hopes converge,
This is the legacy we forge.

The Strains of Time

With ticking clock, our moments fade,
A symphony of choices made.
Each note we play, a memory,
In echoes deep, our destiny.

The sands of time may slip away,
Yet in our hearts, they choose to stay.
In shadows cast by fading light,
We find the strength to face the night.

The gentle strain of life's sweet song,
Reminds us where our souls belong.
In whispered winds, tales intertwine,
A melody amid the pine.

Through laughter's grace and sorrow's ache,
We pave the path for love's own sake.
As seasons change and rivers flow,
We learn to cherish, let things go.

In twilight's glow, we seek the grace,
To dance through time, a warm embrace.
For in each moment's tender chime,
We rise and shine, beyond the grime.

Winds of Transformation

The winds arise, they shift and sway,
They carry dreams, in disarray.
With every gust, a new refrain,
A dance of change, through joy and pain.

Through valleys deep and mountains high,
We feel the winds, we learn to fly.
In whispers soft, they guide our flight,
Through stormy skies, toward the light.

Change is the force that shapes our fate,
In every breath, we cultivate.
With open hearts, we embrace the change,
For life's a canvas, wide and strange.

In every heart, a gust resides,
A force of nature that abides.
To let go of what we hold dear,
Is to find a path, free from fear.

As winds transform, we stand renewed,
In every struggle, we've accrued.
With courage found in winds so bold,
Our stories told, in whispers of gold.

A Tapestry of Unraveled Threads

In patterns rich, our lives unfold,
Threads of stories, new and old.
Each vibrant strand, a voice in time,
A tapestry, both harsh and sublime.

With every weave, a tale is spun,
Of battles fought, of races run.
In colors bright, our sorrows blend,
A vibrant scene with no clear end.

For threads unspooled may seem unclear,
Yet in their chaos, love draws near.
In tangled knots, we find our fate,
A beauty forged, despite the weight.

Each life a thread in grand design,
Together woven, hearts align.
In moments shared, our threads entwine,
A tapestry of love divine.

Through every tear and joyful sigh,
We stitch our hopes, we learn to fly.
In artistry of life, we tread,
This sacred weave, our spirits spread.

The Dance of Shadows and Light

In twilight's gentle embrace,
Shadows weave their soft lace.
Whispers of light flicker near,
Bringing warmth, dispelling fear.

A waltz of forms, entwined and free,
Chasing dreams like leaves from a tree.
Echoes dance on the cool, crisp air,
Painting stories, both bright and rare.

Illuminated by the stars' glow,
Secrets are shared in the flow.
A rhythm that stirs the soul's flight,
Forever bound, shadows and light.

Through the night's enchanting game,
No two dances are the same.
With every twist, a tale begins,
A silent heart where love still spins.

In this realm where night softly sighs,
The dance persists beneath the skies.
A ballet of moments, fleeting yet bright,
Forever cherished, shadows and light.

Ephemeral Whispers of Tomorrow

In the dawn's soft, tender glow,
Promises of future flow.
Ephemeral whispers kiss the breeze,
Carrying dreams like fallen leaves.

Hope dances lightly on the air,
Fleeting moments, beyond compare.
Each breath a spark, a chance to grow,
In the garden of what we sow.

Yesterday's shadows fade away,
Leaving space for a new day.
Each heartbeat a gentle reminder,
Of paths unknown, dreams that bind her.

Embrace the now, let worries cease,
In whispers lie the seeds of peace.
Hold on to visions yet to come,
And let the future's song be sung.

In fleeting time, our worries shrink,
Moments grasped in a single blink.
Eternally onward we chase,
The whispers of tomorrow's grace.

Tracing Roots in Unknown Soil

In the depths of uncharted lands,
Footsteps carve where hope expands.
Each seed sown in fertile ground,
Bears a legacy, profound.

Roots entwine in a dance of fate,
Bridging past and present's gate.
Seeking solace in what we find,
A tapestry of heart and mind.

Beneath the surface, stories hide,
Whispers of those who lived with pride.
Tracing lines back through the years,
Nurturing dreams with silent tears.

In every bloom, a chapter's told,
Of courage, warmth, and hearts so bold.
Through chaos, beauty starts to rise,
In unknown soil, we find our skies.

A journey shared, for all who roam,
In every root, we find a home.
Connected through time, we stand as one,
With every tracing, a new day begun.

The Language of Fluidity

Like waters flowing, ever free,
Embracing each and every spree.
Gestures speak where words might fail,
In currents strong, we set our sail.

A dance of grace on liquid waves,
In every moment, the spirit braves.
Fluid forms that bend and sway,
Navigating night and day.

In the depths where stillness lies,
The heart learns how to rise.
A symphony of ebb and flow,
In tides of time, we learn to grow.

Each ripple tells a tale unspun,
Of battles fought, and victories won.
In every drop, a world unfolds,
A language rich, both fierce and bold.

Through the changes, we become,
A chorus played, a beating drum.
In fluidity, our souls take flight,
Embracing the chaos, chasing the light.

The Echoes of Our Transformation

In the silence, whispers call,
Dreams awaken, shadows fall.
Steps we take, paths unknown,
Each heartbeat, a seed sown.

Time shapes us, like the clay,
Molding nights into the day.
Through the trials, scars reveal,
The beauty in how we feel.

Vows unspoken carve our way,
Lessons learned, here we stay.
Eyes wide open, hearts in flight,
Yearning for the burst of light.

In reflections, truths collide,
Identities worn like a tide.
With each turn, we grow anew,
Resilient, brave, and bold, it's true.

Every echo, every breath,
Celebrates the dance with death.
For in endings, we commence,
A journey rich in recompense.

Shadows of a Shifting Self

Beneath the surface, layers lie,
Whispers thread through the sky.
A mirror's gaze, shows the rift,
In shadows, we learn to shift.

Ghosts of past still linger near,
In the silence, we confront fear.
Awakening the dormant soul,
A search for a deeper goal.

Every heartbeat marks the change,
In the stillness, we rearrange.
The essence of who we might be,
In shadows' dance, wild and free.

Through dark nights and dawning days,
New reflections break the haze.
Each step forward, shedding skin,
Embracing loss, letting win.

In shifting sands, the truth will grow,
Roots entwined in ebb and flow.
With each shadow, we redefine,
The journey ahead, so divine.

The Tides of Change

Waves that crash upon the shore,
Carve the land, forevermore.
In their rhythm, life's embrace,
A dance of time, a sacred space.

With the moon, we rise and fall,
Echoes of an ancient call.
Every shift, a story spun,
In the tides, we are all one.

Moments drift like grains of sand,
Collectively, we understand.
Each heartbeat, an ebb and flow,
Guided by the winds we know.

Seasons change, as do we,
In this vast, awakening sea.
Life unfolds like morning light,
Chasing dreams through day and night.

Let us sail on winds of fate,
Embrace the flow, not hesitate.
For the tides will lead us true,
To the shores where dreams renew.

Fragments of a Forgotten Identity

In dust and echoes, we reside,
Memories where dreams collide.
Fragments scattered in the past,
Shadows linger, fleeting, vast.

Lost in time, we search for stars,
Picking pieces, healing scars.
Voices whisper through the night,
Guiding paths, igniting light.

A puzzle forged from fractured grace,
Each fragment wears a different face.
In the chaos, we find refrain,
A melody in joy and pain.

Through the echoes of who we were,
Rises a song, a gentle stir.
Embracing all that we have been,
Cradling loss, letting love win.

For every shard shows us the way,
To reclaim what's lost, today.
In unity, we stand and sing,
Celebrating every spring.

Faces Beneath the Surface

Whispers of shadows dance at night,
Hidden stories out of sight.
Eyes that glimmer, hearts that ache,
Worn and weary, yet they awake.

Each curve and wrinkle tells of pain,
Echoes of joy, like soft rain.
Years committed to their plight,
Searching for solace, seeking light.

In the silence, dreams unfold,
Tales of courage, truths so bold.
Mirror reflections, fractured views,
Beneath the surface, they diffuse.

Yet in the depths, hope still thrives,
Radiating warmth, where love survives.
Through battles fought, the spirit shines,
Illuminating hearts and minds.

Faces reveal what lies within,
The tender battles, where we begin.
In unity, they strive to stand,
Holding each other, hand in hand.

Ripples of Uncertainty

A stone cast into a tranquil lake,
Waves of doubt begin to shake.
What paths unknown lie ahead?
Questions linger, thoughts widespread.

Each ripple spreads in silent fear,
What if the end is drawing near?
Fragile dreams, so easily swayed,
Hopes that flicker, dimly played.

In shadows cast by fleeting light,
We ponder choices, wrong and right.
Yet through the murk, we strive to see,
A whisper urging us to be.

More than the tremors on the sea,
A surge of faith, a chance to be free.
Through uncertainty, we embrace the fight,
Finding our way back to the light.

Ripples may fade, but not in vain,
Each moment teaches, joy or pain.
In the heart's depth, we gain our ground,
Navigating the lost and found.

Through the Veil of Time

Moments whisper soft and low,
Echoes of the past still flow.
Fleeting shadows, memories wane,
Fragments of joy, stitched with pain.

Beneath the veil, the stories hide,
Tales of lovers, dreams denied.
Through seasons changing, faces fade,
Time, a silent, shifting blade.

Yet in the whispers, wisdom glows,
Lessons learned, as the river flows.
The clock may tick, the sun may rise,
But in our hearts, the truth survives.

Through the veil, we chase the years,
Through laughter shared and silent tears.
In the tapestry of life, we find,
The intertwining of soul and mind.

Glimmers of hope shine through the gloom,
A promise held in futures' bloom.
Together we weave our fateful thread,
Guided by the spirits of the dead.

The Evolution of Togetherness

In the beginning, a spark ignites,
Two souls journey in the night.
Hand in hand, they weave their fate,
In harmony, they resonate.

Through trials faced, their bond does grow,
Lessons learned, hearts in tow.
Each moment shared, a piece in place,
A dance of love, a timeless grace.

With every change, they learn to bend,
Cultivating trust that will not end.
Evolving gently, through each stage,
Writing their story on life's page.

Through laughter, tears, they stay entwined,
Facing storms with hearts aligned.
In the fabric of life, stitched tight,
The beauty of love shines ever bright.

Together they stand as seasons shift,
An endless journey, a cherished gift.
The evolution of hearts so true,
Together forever, in all they do.

Unraveling at the Edges

Threads of silence slowly fray,
Whispers lost in shades of gray.
Fingers trace the fading seams,
Hope hangs delicately on dreams.

Moments vivid, yet they slide,
Winds of change, a restless tide.
Memories like shadows blend,
A journey without a clear end.

Glimmers fade, yet spark a light,
Casting shadows through the night.
In the chaos, peace takes root,
Finding strength in fragile fruit.

Echoes of what once was here,
Trails of laughter, paths of fear.
Unraveling as time unfolds,
A tapestry of stories told.

In the stillness, hope abides,
Through the storm, the heart decides.
Threads may break but won't erase,
A love that time cannot displace.

The Path of Our Rebirth

Amidst the ashes, flowers bloom,
From darkened streets to brightened rooms.
In every loss, a chance to rise,
New beginnings in the skies.

We carve our fate with tender hands,
Write our stories on shifting sands.
Together we embrace the dawn,
Dreams awaken, fears are gone.

Steps retraced through fields of gold,
Lessons learned, and tales retold.
With every heartbeat, we immerse,
Finding strength in each reverse.

Winds of change will guide our way,
Past the shadows of yesterday.
In each heartbeat, we reclaim,
The very essence of our name.

Through stormy nights, we stand as one,
Until the rising of the sun.
In our rebirth, we ignite,
The flames of courage burning bright.

Tangled Roots and Wings

Beneath the surface, roots entwine,
Stories hidden, rich and fine.
From earth we rise, both strong and free,
Nature's bond, our symphony.

Each branch extends to touch the sky,
In flight we learn to dare, to try.
With tangled roots, we seek the light,
Finding wisdom in our flight.

Gravity pulls, yet dreams take flight,
In the darkness, we find our light.
Through crackling leaves and rustling trees,
Navigate life's flowing breeze.

In every storm, the strong will bend,
With roots that twist and never end.
Capable hearts, we seek to soar,
Embrace the world with open doors.

Understanding lives deep within,
Wings unfurled, we begin again.
From tangled roots, we form our wings,
And through the course, our spirit sings.

Echoing Voices in the Stillness

In the quiet, voices call,
Softest murmurs rise and fall.
Shadows dance without a sound,
In the stillness, truths abound.

Echoes linger from the past,
Memories like shadows cast.
Through the silence, wisdom flows,
A gentle breeze that softly blows.

Fragments of a whispered prayer,
Resonating in the air.
In the calm, our hearts align,
Seeking peace, divine, divine.

Moments stretch, with time to breathe,
In stillness, we find reprieve.
Voices stitched through time and space,
Bind our spirits, hold our grace.

In this place where echoes sing,
Love and hope forever cling.
Through the stillness, we transcend,
In every heartbeat, find a friend.

The Elegy of What Was

In shadows where memories linger,
Ghosts of laughter softly sigh.
Time's passage, a silent singer,
Whispers of an age gone by.

Fading echoes, bittersweet,
Photographs worn at the edges.
Moments lost, yet feel complete,
Life's song across the hedges.

Each heartbeat, a torn reflection,
Carved in stone, the past remains.
A tapestry of connection,
Woven in joy and pains.

Dusty roads and wilted flowers,
Remind me of what we shared.
Time may steal its final powers,
Yet love is always bared.

In the twilight, we still dance,
To melodies of old.
In memory's tender trance,
The stories that we told.

Creatures of Evolution

Once we thrived on ocean's crest,
Primitive forms, a spark of light.
Journeyed forth, a timeless quest,
In shadows deep of day and night.

Scales turned to feathers, truth be told,
Through ages dark, we learned to soar.
Pushing boundaries, bold and bold,
The dance of life forevermore.

Each heartbeat fuels the fervent change,
Adaptation's whispers guide our way.
In nature's hand, we feel the strange,
Embracing night, we greet the day.

From the depths of trees we rise,
Tales of resilience intertwine.
Evolution's blessing, our prize,
In every being, pure design.

Together we weave a vibrant thread,
Of life's creations, wild and wide.
In unity, all fears are shed,
In the pulse of time, we bide.

A Palette of Becoming

With every brush, a tale unfolds,
Colors blend and dance with grace.
In strokes of dreams, the heart beholds,
Visions of a boundless space.

Reds ignite the fire of dawn,
Blues flow like water from the skies.
Greens embrace the earth's soft lawn,
Each hue a bridge to silent cries.

Creativity's breath inspires,
Transforming grief to joy anew.
In the chaos, beauty tires,
Finding peace in shades we brew.

Each canvas bears a whispered name,
Of souls who dared to break the mold.
In vibrant light, we stake our claim,
As stories in pigments told.

A palette rich with every shade,
Of laughter, love, and fleeting sighs.
In art, the heart can never fade,
Eternal under changing skies.

The Pulse of Transformation

Within the stillness, life beats strong,
A rhythm woven into the night.
From shadows deep, we rise along,
With whispered hope, we claim our light.

The seasons shift, the earth awakes,
In cycles vast, we find our way.
Each moment breathes, the fabric shakes,
As dawn ignites the break of day.

Through trials faced, our strength is found,
Transforming fears into the flame.
A heartbeat echoes, profound sound,
An anthem played, we rise, the same.

In every choice, a path unfolds,
An endless dance of give and take.
With open hearts, we seek, behold,
The beauty born from all we make.

Together in this changing tide,
We shape our future, hand in hand.
In every pulse, our dreams reside,
A symphony across the land.

When Silence Speaks Our Names

In quiet halls where shadows dwell,
The echoes of our stories swell.
Each whispered thought, a soft refrain,
In silence deep, we speak our names.

Through muted sighs, the heart reveals,
The truths concealed, the pain that heals.
As time unfolds, we learn to claim,
The hidden dreams that bear our names.

The stillness wraps like woven cloth,
Embracing all that we have sought.
In every pause, a world to tame,
When silence speaks, it calls our names.

A potent force, this quiet grace,
That nudges us to find our place.
In sacred chants, we find our fame,
As silence boldly speaks our names.

So listen close, for in the hush,
Live tales of love, of dreams that rush.
And in the calm, like love's sweet flame,
We'll find the strength to voice our names.

Unfolding Layers of Identity

Beneath the skin, a story lies,
Each layer speaks, through lows and highs.
From roots to branches, we explore,
A tapestry we can't ignore.

In every mark, a path we trace,
The pieces fit, a complex face.
Our histories, entwined like vines,
Unfold the growth through passing times.

Through trials faced and dreams once sown,
We gather strength and seeds we've grown.
With every step, we find our way,
Embracing what the heart must say.

The masks we wear, they shape our view,
Reflecting shades of old and new.
In myriad forms, we come alive,
Unfolding layers where truths thrive.

From whispers shared to shouts of joy,
In every voice, a song to buoy.
As we connect, our hearts ignite,
Unfolding layers reveals the light.

The Tapestry of Change

Threads of time weave stories bright,
Each stitch a whisper, day and night.
In colors bold, and shades of grey,
The tapestry of change holds sway.

With every twist, we learn to bend,
In every knot, a chance to mend.
Through winding paths, we find our way,
A graceful dance where hopes can play.

From roots to stars, a cosmic thread,
With every challenge that we've ever shed.
Together strong, we rise, we fall,
A tapestry that weaves us all.

When seasons shift, we find the spark,
In every ending, a brand new arc.
As we embrace the ebb and flow,
The tapestry of change will grow.

With open hearts, we brave the storm,
In every change, a chance to form.
In colors bright, we boldly claim,
The tapestry of change, our aim.

Whispers of the Forgotten Past

In shadows deep, the echoes fade,
Whispers linger where dreams once laid.
Each tale a sigh, a voice unheard,
In silence do, the past assert.

Forgotten truths on brittle leaves,
In ancient woods, the heart believes.
The tales of old, they softly call,
In whispered tones, they rise, they fall.

As time drifts by, the stories blend,
In every heart, the forgotten mend.
With gentle hands, we weave the lore,
To honor those who came before.

In every heartbeat, echoes stay,
A tapestry of yesterday.
In memory's breath, forged to last,
The whispers of the forgotten past.

So let us listen, let us hear,
The voices soft and crystal clear.
In every tale, a light will cast,
The whispers of the forgotten past.

A Dance of Shattered Dreams

In twilight's grip, we parted ways,
With whispered hopes and silent cries.
The fragments of our laughing days,
Now dance in shadows, lost goodbyes.

A melody of what could be,
Echoes softly through the night.
In broken chords, our history,
Plays on, a bittersweet delight.

Dreams once bright, now turned to dust,
Twirl 'neath stars, a haunting waltz.
Yet, in the chaos, find the trust,
That once united, life exalts.

We twirled through fields of wildflowers,
And grasped the sun with tender hands.
Though time has stolen peaceful hours,
Our spirits linger where love stands.

No longer bound by dreams forlorn,
We rise, reborn, in starlit skies.
In dancing shadows, hearts are sworn,
To cherish all that never dies.

As Time Altered Our Paths

Moments wandered, shifted sands,
You turned away, I looked ahead.
We threaded through life's fickle strands,
Each choice a word left unsaid.

In time's embrace, we learned to bend,
Like willows swaying with the breeze.
What seemed the start grew to an end,
Yet still, our hearts find subtle peace.

The winding roads we each have trod,
Lead to places unforeseen.
We walked with faith, though oft we nod,
At changing fates in gentle scenes.

Through laughter shared and silent tears,
We found the beauty in the chase.
The weight of love, through all the years,
Is woven deep without a trace.

As time paints stories on our souls,
We'll cherish every breath we take.
With every shift, our journey rolls,
In changing light, our hearts awake.

Beyond the Horizon of Us

The sun dips low, our shadows blend,
As day surrenders to the night.
In silence, promises ascend,
While stars ignite the sky's delight.

We chased the dreams that slipped away,
Across the oceans, vast and wide.
With whispers carried on the spray,
Our souls entwined, we turned the tide.

Beyond the curve of what we know,
Awaits a realm of endless skies.
With every step, new seeds we sow,
Embracing truths, as love defies.

In twilight's glow, we find our dawn,
The whispers of a future near.
What once felt lost, now brightly drawn,
In every smile, we conquer fear.

Together, we will rise and soar,
Across horizons yet unseen.
With love as map and heart the core,
We journey forth, a sacred dream.

The Alchemy of Experience

In life's vast cauldron, lessons brew,
Each moment sparks a brand new fate.
Through trials faced and storms we flew,
The heart reveals what time creates.

We gather treasures from our tears,
And polish pain with gentle care.
What shatters falls to elevate,
The strength we build, the love we share.

A tapestry of joy and sorrow,
We weave with threads of laughter, grief.
Through every dawn, we shape tomorrow,
Turning loss to bright belief.

The alchemy of what we've known,
Turns shadows into beams of light.
Each scar a seed, each truth a stone,
Transforms our path into pure flight.

In every breath, the stories blend,
What seems the end, sparks something bright.
With every turn, we will transcend,
Embracing life, our hearts ignite.

The Journey of Shattered Mirrors

In shards of glass, reflections fade,
Each piece reveals a path unmade.
The journey winds through cracks and light,
A maze of hopes that spark the night.

We gather dreams from mountains steep,
In broken whispers, promises keep.
A tapestry of pain and grace,
The mirror's truth, a haunting face.

Through every splinter, lessons learned,
With every heartache, love returned.
We navigate the hurt and joy,
In shattered forms, our spirits buoy.

The journey flows like rivers wide,
Embracing change, we do not hide.
In every crack, a chance to grow,
In every tear, a river's flow.

Through shattered mirrors, visions clear,
We chase the light, dissolve the fear.
In fractured paths, we find our way,
From brokenness, we learn to sway.

Dance of the Evolving Heart

In rhythms soft, the heart does sway,
With every note, we shape the day.
A pulse of life, a tender beat,
In every dance, our souls complete.

Through changing steps, the seasons turn,
With every leap, new passions burn.
The heart expands with every glide,
In fluid movements, dreams collide.

We twirl in shadows, embrace the light,
In every spin, we take our flight.
The dance evolves, a living art,
In freedom found, we play our part.

With every sigh, the moment grows,
In silent whispers, love still flows.
The rhythm changes, we adapt,
With open hearts, there's no mishap.

As time will weave our stories true,
We'll waltz through nights, as lovers do.
In every gesture, beauty seen,
The dance of life, forever keen.

Beyond the Familiar Horizon

The dawn breaks soft on distant shores,
With every gaze, adventure soars.
Beyond the edge where skies collide,
A world awaits, where dreams reside.

In whispered winds, new tales are spun,
A call to venture, journeys begun.
Beyond the hills, the valleys wide,
In every heart, a spark inside.

We walk the paths less traveled first,
With every step, quenched is our thirst.
In every shadow, light will gleam,
As we pursue a daring dream.

Together, we will chase the stars,
Unlock the secrets held in jars.
Beyond the horizon's curved embrace,
We look ahead, a daring race.

In twilight's glow, our spirits rise,
With open hearts, we claim the skies.
Beyond the familiar, we will roam,
In lands unknown, we'll build our home.

The Shape of Our Tomorrow

In every choice, the future forms,
A canvas stretched by dreams and storms.
With colors bright, we paint each day,
In gentle strokes, we find our way.

A vision shared, our hopes align,
In every heartbeat, love's design.
Together, we'll create and mold,
The stories of our lives unfold.

In laughter's echo, joy will thrive,
Through trials faced, we learn to strive.
The shape of what is yet to come,
With every challenge, we become.

In unity, we rise anew,
With every dream, a brighter view.
The world ahead is ours to take,
In every dawn, our hearts awake.

In whispered hopes, the future gleams,
With courage found in waking dreams.
The shape of tomorrow, bold and bright,
In our embrace, we hold the light.

The Mirage of Becoming

In shadows cast by dreams untold,
We wander paths both bright and cold.
Each step a choice, a path unknown,
A mirage seen, a truth overthrown.

With every breath, the pages turn,
Lessons learned, and hearts that yearn.
We chase reflections in the sand,
Yet find ourselves in shifting land.

The faces change, but souls remain,
In every joy, in every pain.
Through fleeting moments, we embrace,
A journey bound, yet free in space.

The mirage glimmers, beckons near,
An echo soft, both far and clear.
With open hearts, we dare to see,
The beauty in this mystery.

So here we stand, in twilight's glow,
Embracing all that we may know.
In this mirage of becoming new,
We find ourselves in shades of true.

Cascading into New Realms

Like waters tumbling, pure and bright,
We flow through valleys, into light.
Each drop a moment, swift and free,
Cascading forth in harmony.

The currents pull, a whispered call,
Into new realms where shadows fall.
We dance with fate, in swirling streams,
Creating life from fleeting dreams.

Through twists and turns, our spirits rise,
In every challenge, a new surprise.
We learn to bend, we learn to sway,
As water shapes the course of day.

With every plunge, we shed the old,
Embracing change, both brave and bold.
In nature's flow, we find our way,
Cascading into bright array.

So let us dive, our hearts awake,
Into the dance of give and take.
For life is but a flowing stream,
A cascade where we dare to dream.

The Spiral Dance of Life

In circles wide, we spin and twirl,
A dance of joy, a sacred whirl.
Each step a beat, a rhythm strong,
In the spiral dance, we all belong.

With laughter shared, we lift the veil,
Embracing stories we tell and hail.
United in this vibrant spree,
The spiral leads us, wild and free.

As seasons change, we learn to sway,
To ebb and flow with night and day.
With courage found, we face the storm,
In every twist, we feel the warm.

The spiral whispers secrets deep,
In every turn, our hearts we keep.
We journey forth, hand in hand,
In life's great dance, we take a stand.

So let us twirl, let spirits soar,
In this sublime and endless chore.
For life's a dance, a sacred rite,
The spiral's grace, our pure delight.

The Color Palette of Our Lives

Across the canvas, hues collide,
With every stroke, our hearts confide.
In vibrant shades, our stories blend,
The palette speaks where words may end.

From warmest reds to cool cerulean,
Each color tells of joy and pain.
In every line, a tale unfolds,
A vivid truth in wisdom bold.

We gather shades from life's embrace,
With laughter bright, and sorrow's grace.
The brush of time strokes soft and true,
Creating shades both old and new.

In depth and light, the shadows play,
Reflecting all that fades away.
But still we paint, with every breath,
A masterpiece beyond all death.

So let us choose our colors bright,
And paint our dreams in purest light.
For in this art, our lives arrive,
The color palette keeps us alive.

The Pulse of New Beginnings

A seed breaks through the soil,
In sunlight's gentle embrace,
Whispers of dreams ignite,
Time begins its chase.

Each dawn brings a soft light,
Carving paths in the dew,
Moments of hope take flight,
A canvas fresh and new.

With wings that long to soar,
The heart beats loud and clear,
New chapters yet to explore,
A world without fear.

Each step a rhythm learned,
Like dancers on the stage,
A fire inside us burned,
Together, we engage.

Life flows like a river,
Through valleys and up hills,
In every gentle quiver,
The promise always fills.

Poised Between Past and Future

A bridge spans over time,
Where memories softly sway,
With echoes of the climb,
And dawns of yesterday.

In shadows we find light,
A tethered heart does ache,
With every whispered night,
We learn what it can take.

The compass holds its true,
Guiding steps down the line,
Beneath the moon's soft hue,
Exists both yours and mine.

Hope clings like morning mist,
To visions yet unknown,
In every breath, a twist,
The seeds of change have grown.

Time dances in a swirl,
A balance on the edge,
We weave the dreams that curl,
A life we choose to pledge.

Chasing Lost Visions

In twilight's fading glow,
Ghosts of hopes appear,
They shimmer soft and slow,
Not far, yet oh so near.

With whispers on the breeze,
They call out from the past,
A melody that frees,
Reminders made to last.

Each shadow tells a tale,
Of dreams once held so tight,
In the heart they prevail,
Flickering in the night.

Through labyrinths we run,
In search of what was lost,
Chasing the fading sun,
Awake to bear the cost.

Yet visions guide our way,
Through corridors of time,
In every dusk and day,
A promise: hope will climb.

The Emergence of Yesterday's Ghosts

In silence, they draw near,
Faint whispers in the dark,
They carry old held fear,
Yet breathe a hopeful spark.

In shadows of the past,
Fleeting as they roam,
The echoes hold steadfast,
Reminding us of home.

Each memory takes shape,
A tapestry of grace,
Unlocking every gate,
To time's long-held embrace.

With every tear we weave,
The fabric of our lore,
A chance to truly grieve,
And heal what we ignore.

So rise, ye gentle shades,
In dawn's sweet golden light,
From whispers to cascades,
Let yesterday take flight.

Embracing the Unknown

In shadows deep where silence lies,
We find the strength to reach for skies.
Heartbeats echo, fears unwind,
With open arms, new dreams we find.

A path uncharted, steps unsure,
Yet in our hearts, we feel allure.
The night may creep, but stars will glow,
Guiding us where we dare to go.

Through tangled woods, we forge ahead,
Seeking the truth in words unsaid.
Each twist and turn, a lesson learned,
With every choice, a fire burned.

Courage blooms in every heart,
In the unknown, we play our part.
With every breath, a journey starts,
Embracing life with open hearts.

So let us chase the hidden light,
Wrap ourselves in velvet night.
For in the dark, we come to see,
The beauty of what's yet to be.

Skeletons of Our Past

In dusty rooms, the shadows rest,
Whispers echo, secrets pressed.
Fractured frames of what we knew,
Stories linger, old and true.

Bones of history rise with grace,
Marking time, a silent place.
Memories dance in faded halls,
Ancestral voices softly call.

The weight of years, it haunts our stride,
Yet in their depths, we learn and bide.
From ashes, strength, we do reclaim,
The scars we bear, they tell our name.

Threads of gold woven through pain,
In every loss, we find a gain.
Skeletons teach, they guide our way,
Embracing shadows, come what may.

We rise anew from dust and time,
Building futures, hearts in rhyme.
With every step, we break the mold,
From ruins, courage to be bold.

Whispers of a New Dawn

In tender hues, the morning breaks,
Awakening dreams, the world remakes.
Birds in chorus, sweet refrain,
Sing of hope after the rain.

Winds of change, they kiss the land,
A gentle touch, a guiding hand.
Each day unfolds a canvas bright,
Painting shadows with new light.

The past retreats, a fading song,
In every heartbeat, we belong.
With every tear, a seed is sown,
A promise held in courage grown.

Morning's veil, a soft embrace,
In twilight's wake, we find our place.
With every dawn, a chance is born,
To rise again, the spirit's sworn.

So breathe in deep, the fresh and clear,
The whispers catch, inviting cheer.
For after night, the sun will shine,
And fill our hearts with love divine.

Metamorphosis in Motion

In the stillness, change begins,
A dance of life, where hope spins.
Caterpillars dream of skies,
In quiet hearts, the spirit flies.

With every struggle that we face,
We find the strength to seek our place.
Transformations, fierce and sweet,
Creating wings beneath our feet.

The world awakens, colors bright,
A canvas stretched with pure delight.
From seed to bloom, we journey far,
Reaching high, we touch the stars.

In every heartbeat, change we feel,
Breaking shells, a soul revealed.
Resilience grows in every tear,
Metamorphosis, our path is clear.

So let us dance through storms of time,
With every fall, we learn to climb.
Embrace the shift, the wild notion,
Of life's sweet art, in constant motion.

The Voyage of Weaving Dreams

On a sail of silver threads, we glide,
Through realms where whispered secrets hide.
Each stitch a story, every knot a chance,
We weave our hopes in a timeless dance.

The stars align, guiding our way,
In the quiet moonlight, dreams softly sway.
With every ebb, our spirits soar,
A tapestry of wishes, forevermore.

The waves of fate will crash and roar,
Yet in our hearts, we find the shore.
Each dream a wave, rising high,
Together we'll reach for the boundless sky.

With hands entwined, we chart our course,
Through storms and calm, we find our force.
In every fiber, love's embrace,
United we stand, in this sacred space.

So take the helm, let courage guide,
For in this voyage, we shall confide.
Through realms unseen, we boldly sail,
Together we'll write our own sweet tale.

Meeting at the Crossroads

Two paths diverged under the trees,
Whispers of fate danced in the breeze.
Eyes locked in a timeless trance,
In this moment, we take a chance.

Hands trembling, the choice laid bare,
A fork in the road, hearts stripped of care.
With every breath, the world stood still,
What lies ahead, a thrill to fulfill.

Words unspoken, yet understood,
In the silence, we find what's good.
Two souls meeting, as stars align,
In this embrace, our worlds entwine.

Every step forward, a leap of faith,
Together we journey, whatever awaits.
With eyes wide open, onward we tread,
In this dance, there's nothing to dread.

So let us wander, hand in hand,
At the crossroads, together we stand.
With dreams as our guide, we'll carve our way,
In the light of hope, we choose to stay.

Sprouts from Parched Earth

In a barren land where silence reigned,
Seeds of hope lie unrestrained.
With drops of rain, a miracle blooms,
Colors awaken, dispelling gloom.

Roots dig deep, reaching for the light,
Cracks in the ground transform the night.
Each tender shoot breaks free with grace,
A testament of life, a warm embrace.

Nature whispers of journeys new,
Through drought and struggle, the heart stays true.
With every petal, a story unfolds,
Of resilience and strength, a treasure untold.

The sun rises high, casting its glow,
Life pushes forward, continuing to grow.
Each sprout a promise, each bud a dream,
In unity with earth, we find our theme.

So let us cherish this vibrant burst,
In the depths of despair, let hope be first.
From parched earth, a symphony sings,
In nature's chorus, we find our wings.

Sandcastle Dreams in an Ocean of Change

On the shore, where waves kiss sand,
We build our dreams with careful hands.
Each grain a memory, sculpted with care,
In the light of sunset, magic fills the air.

The tide rolls in, a gentle caress,
Washing away worries, leaving us blessed.
With every wave, our lives rearrange,
Yet in this moment, we embrace the change.

Castles rise tall, adorned with shells,
Stories of laughter, of whispers and yells.
As the ocean sings, we stand side by side,
In this dance of dreams, we take the ride.

But the tide knows not of our sweet plans,
It takes with grace what the heart spans.
As castles crumble, we find the core,
In the heart of chaos, we crave for more.

So let the waves come, let them play,
In this ocean of change, we'll find our way.
With each new dawn, we'll start anew,
In sandcastle dreams, love will shine through.

When Time Wove Us Differently

In the cradle of days gone by,
Threads of laughter softly wove,
Moments danced like fireflies,
Shadows whispered secrets we strove.

Hours spun into fragile lace,
Gentle breath of fading light,
Paths diverged in tangled grace,
Yet hearts held tight to dreams so bright.

Seasons turned with quiet ease,
Turning tides, a silent drift,
Through the winds, we learned to seize,
Time's embrace, our precious gift.

Now we stand in twilight's glow,
Bridges built on yesterday,
Eager hearts, still want to grow,
Woven visions guide our way.

In the fabric of our past,
Stitched with hope and ancient signs,
Though the threads may fray and last,
Love endures, through space and time.

The Masks We Wear

In the mirror, faces shift,
Layers crafted to protect,
Hiding truths that often drift,
We wear smiles, yet feel defect.

Curtains drawn on fragile hearts,
Jesters don their painted grins,
Playing roles as life imparts,
Underneath, where silence spins.

In crowded rooms, we stand alone,
Whispers caught in laughter's chase,
Searching for a truth to own,
Longing to be seen, not traced.

At dusk we peel our colors back,
And find the voices softly stir,
In authenticity's sweet crack,
We learn to dance, not just confer.

With every mask, a lesson learned,
The weights we carry, shared by all,
In our depths, the fire burns,
Revealing core beneath the hall.

Seeds of Evolution

Buried deep in fertile ground,
Silent hopes await their time,
Each a tale yet to be found,
Nature's rhythm, sweet and prime.

Raindrops kissed the parched earth's skin,
Sunlight stretched across the fields,
In the dark, where growth begins,
Life awakens, gently yields.

Roots entwined beneath the layer,
Tales of struggle, strength, and grace,
Through the toil and loving care,
Blooming dreams in sacred space.

With each cycle, change unfolds,
Colors splash, and scents entwine,
In the story that nature holds,
Life evolves, a dance divine.

From the smallest seed we rise,
Reaching up toward the vast skies,
In the heart of change, we find,
Life's true essence intertwined.

The Alchemy of Us

In the crucible of our days,
Elements of us combine,
Forged in trust, a golden blaze,
From chaos born, a design.

Hearts entwined in sacred fire,
Melting barriers of old,
In the heat, we find our desire,
Transforming lead to vibrant gold.

With every challenge, we refine,
Sparks of laughter light the way,
Between our souls, a brilliant line,
The alchemy of love at play.

Like potions stirred in whispered night,
Secrets shared in quiet hour,
We blend our dreams, taking flight,
From stardust drawn, we wield our power.

In the end, it's clear to see,
What once was separate now is fused,
Together we create our spree,
In this magic, we are bruised, yet amused.

Threading Through the Labyrinth

In the shadows, whispers dwell,
Echoes call, a distant spell.
Through corridors of twisted time,
We seek the truth in every rhyme.

Winding paths of choices made,
Each turn a dance, decisions laid.
Steps echo soft on ancient stone,
Guiding hearts to find their own.

A flicker glows in depths of night,
Illuminating paths to light.
Fear not the maze, embrace the quest,
In winding halls, we are blessed.

Find the thread that leads you home,
Through tangled webs, we learn to roam.
The labyrinth holds both pain and grace,
Each twist and turn, a sacred space.

With every choice, a story's spun,
In the labyrinth, we are one.
In threads of hope, we dare to weave,
Through darkened paths, we shall believe.

The Weaving of New Realities

Colors blend in twilight's hue,
Dreams and fears, they start anew.
Each thread a wish, each knot a tale,
In destiny's loom, we shall prevail.

Hands entwined in sacred art,
Stitching moments from the heart.
Through laughter, tears, and whispered fears,
We craft tomorrow, year by year.

Patterns shift in the cosmic dance,
Every chance a fleeting glance.
Weaving visions, bright and bold,
In fabric rich, our lives unfold.

Threads of fate pull tight and far,
Guiding us beneath each star.
In every weave, a promise lies,
A tapestry of fresh sunrise.

Together we shape the world so wide,
In unity, we take our stride.
On this canvas, our stories blend,
Through weaving dreams, we'll never end.

Eclipsed by Memory

Shadows dance on walls of time,
Fading echoes, lost in rhyme.
Memories linger, sweet and bitter,
In the heart, their glow gets dimmer.

Moments flash like fleeting light,
Lost in whispers of the night.
Each memory a fragile thread,
Connected to all we've left unsaid.

When silence falls, the past awakes,
In the deep, the stillness shakes.
Through veils of time, we reach and yearn,
In shadows, the candle burns.

Fragments glimmer, shards of glass,
Timeless ghosts, they come to pass.
Eclipsed by time's relentless tide,
In memory's grasp, we must abide.

With every change, we hold them near,
Each story we weave shines crystal clear.
In the darkness, a light remains,
Eclipsed but bright, through joys and pains.

Footprints on the Edge of Tomorrow

Each step we take on fragile ground,
Leaves a mark where dreams are found.
Walking paths yet to be drawn,
In the light of the breaking dawn.

Whispers call from the unknown,
In our hearts, seeds of hope are sown.
Future waits just out of sight,
A canvas blank, awaiting light.

With every choice, we carve our fate,
In the echoes, we resonate.
From the edges of time and space,
Footprints lead to a sacred place.

Feel the pulse of what could be,
In every step, we learn to see.
The horizon stretches wide and free,
A promise held in unity.

Together we walk, hand in hand,
Across the shores of shifting sand.
Each footprint tells a tale so grand,
On the edge of tomorrow, we stand.

Reflections of a Unfolding Story

In echoes soft, we find our place,
Each whispered thought, a gentle trace.
The moments dance, like fleeting light,
As shadows play, we claim the night.

With every step, the past unfolds,
A tapestry of tales retold.
In every heart, a spark ignites,
To weave the dreams in starry nights.

Through laughter's grace and sorrow's cheer,
We gather strength, we persevere.
Each chapter close, a new begun,
Together still, we are as one.

The pages turn, the ink remains,
A portrait drawn of joys and pains.
We'll write our fate, with every breath,
In love's embrace, we'll conquer death.

So come, dear friend, let echoes soar,
In life's vast tale, there lies much more.
With open hearts, we share the stage,
In this unfolding, turning page.

The Threads of Our Legacy

In every choice, a thread we weave,
A story rich, in hearts believed.
Each bond we form, a tapestry,
Of hopes and dreams, in unity.

Like rivers flow, our paths entwined,
The marks we leave, forever bind.
In laughter's joy and sorrow's sigh,
The threads connect, as seasons fly.

Through whispers soft, our tales are spun,
In cherished moments, we are one.
The strength we share in trials faced,
In every heartbeat, love embraced.

As echoes fade, our legacy,
Is held in souls that long to be.
With kindness sown, and wisdom shared,
The future shines, for we have cared.

So let us plant these seeds of grace,
In every heart, a sacred space.
Together strong, we forge the way,
The threads of love will never fray.

Farewell to Yesterday

When twilight falls, we bid goodbye,
To moments lost, where memories lie.
In whispered tones, the past we greet,
Yet forward bound, we won't retreat.

The dreams once dreamt, now fade to night,
With every dawn, new hopes take flight.
In letting go, we find, we grow,
Embracing change, the tides will flow.

With each goodbye, a lesson learned,
In sorrow's grasp, our passions burned.
For every tear that falls from eyes,
New laughter waits beneath the skies.

So hold the past, but don't be bound,
In freedom's song, our strength is found.
For every end, a start appears,
In echoes soft, we forge the years.

With open hearts, we face the morn,
With courage strong, a will reborn.
In the light of hope, we'll dance away,
To welcome new with each new day.

The Art of Becoming

In every step, we find our way,
A journey grand, come what may.
With open arms, we greet the dawn,
In every struggle, we are drawn.

The flicker glows, within us bright,
A flame of dreams that dares to fight.
In shadowed paths, we learn to rise,
To shed our fears and touch the skies.

With every heartbeat, we transform,
In gentle storms, our spirits warm.
The art of growth is never still,
It shaping hearts, a sacred will.

So dance with joy, embrace the sea,
For in our souls, we are set free.
With every breath, we take our place,
In life's great art, a boundless grace.

In every change, we find the spark,
A tapestry of light from dark.
Together strong, we bloom and grow,
The art of becoming, all we know.

Echoes of Transformation

In whispers soft, we find our way,
New paths unfold, in light of day.
The past, a guide, yet not our chain,
We rise anew, from loss and gain.

With every step, the earth we tread,
Stories linger, words unsaid.
In shadows cast, our visions gleam,
Transformed by hope, we dare to dream.

The seasons change, as we evolve,
In heart and mind, our selves resolve.
Embracing change, we shed our skin,
And dance with life, where dreams begin.

Unfurling wings, like birds in flight,
We soar above, into the light.
Echoes call from days of yore,
A symphony we can't ignore.

With every echo, wisdom grows,
Through ups and downs, the journey shows.
In transformation, we become,
A chorus strong, a beating drum.

Shadows of Our Former Selves

In twilight's glow, the shadows play,
Reminders of our yesterday.
Fleeting forms, like ghosts they drift,
Whispering secrets, time's gentle gift.

We move through realms, both lost and found,
In echoes deep, where dreams abound.
The specters loom, but do not bind,
They teach us grace, in heart and mind.

With every step, we confront the past,
In its embrace, our truths are cast.
Though shadows linger, we light the way,
Through fears and doubts, we find our stay.

As memories weave, both dark and bright,
We stitch a tapestry of light.
Emerging strong from what we've been,
Shadows dance, but we break in.

With every whisper of our lore,
We hold the keys, we can explore.
The shadows fade, till they dissolve,
In love and light, we find resolve.

The Shifting Canvas of Us

A canvas vast, our stories blend,
In colors bold, they twist and bend.
Each brushstroke speaks of tales untold,
Of love, of loss, of dreams of gold.

With every hue, new worlds emerge,
A dance of fate, a life on verge.
Textures shift in the hands of time,
Creating art, both crude and prime.

We sketch our lives, with hope and fear,
In vibrant strokes, we persevere.
The palette deepens, rich and wide,
In every layer, we must decide.

Through trials faced and moments bright,
The canvas speaks in day and night.
The shifting form of who we are,
A masterpiece, beneath the stars.

Unveiled at last, our hearts laid bare,
In each design, a tender care.
A world transformed, not just for show,
In every shade, we choose to grow.

Metamorphosis in Starlight

Beneath the vast and sparkling sky,
We seek the place where dreams can fly.
In starlit whispers, change begins,
A dance of fate, where hope still spins.

The night unfolds its velvet cloak,
In silence shared, our spirits provoke.
With every twinkle, secrets lie,
We shed old skins, and learn to fly.

Through cosmic paths, our hearts align,
In rhythms soft, we intertwine.
The universe sings a lullaby,
To guide us forth, as we comply.

Each moment sparks a flame anew,
In starlight's glow, our fears subdue.
A metamorphosis, pure and fair,
In hidden realms, we learn to care.

In every heartbeat, magic swells,
A journey told in starlit spells.
We rise like phoenix, fierce and free,
Transforming all, eternally.

Mosaic of Our New Horizons

Colors blend in twilight's hue,
New paths await, where dreams break through.
Each step a story, yet untold,
In unity, our hearts unfold.

Stars above, a guiding light,
Whispers soft in the calm of night.
Together we weave, hand in hand,
On this vibrant, uncharted land.

Hope ignites in every heart,
From fragments, we each play a part.
With courage, we rise and soar,
Painting futures forevermore.

Through trials, our spirits grow,
In the dance of the ebb and flow.
We stand strong, in truth's embrace,
Creating beauty in this space.

Mosaic dreams in radiant light,
Guiding us through day and night.
With every piece, we become whole,
United in spirit, body, and soul.

Lost and Found in Between

In the silence, echoes breathe,
Memories linger, gently seethe.
Moments lived yet hard to trace,
Fragments lost in time and space.

Paths we wandered, left behind,
Seek the threads that still unwind.
In shadows deep, truths are found,
Where souls whisper, softly bound.

Hearts collide in hidden ways,
In the twilight of uncertain days.
Lost and found, we meet the dawn,
In the space where love is drawn.

Every heartbeat, a silent plea,
In the gaps of you and me.
We rise from ashes, reborn anew,
In the spaces that once we knew.

So let us linger here and stay,
In the moments that fade away.
For in between, we come alive,
In this dance, we shall survive.

Fragments of a Shared Story

Pages torn, yet stories blend,
Voices echo, hearts they mend.
Threads of laughter, threads of pain,
In every sun, in every rain.

Whispers of youth, a time long past,
Dreams that shimmer, shadows cast.
Each fragment holds a piece of grace,
Together we find our rightful place.

In the tapestry of nights and days,
Weaving hope in countless ways.
With every stitch, our souls align,
In this story, yours and mine.

Gather round, let hearts convene,
In the spaces that lie between.
Together we stand, undeterred,
In every note, our song is heard.

Fragments shine like stars above,
Binding stories hand in glove.
In every tale, a truth we see,
In this narrative, we are free.

Shifting Ground Beneath Our Feet

The earth trembles, a subtle sigh,
Underneath the vast, wide sky.
In the moment, we lose our way,
Yet hope lingers, come what may.

Paths uncertain, futures vague,
We seek solace, hearts must brave.
In the chaos, find the calm,
Amidst the storm, a healing balm.

Roots entwined, we stand as one,
Facing shadows, facing sun.
In the tremors, we discover,
Strength in heart, in one another.

The ground shifts, but we remain,
Navigating joy and pain.
With every shake, we learn to dance,
In the rhythm of happenstance.

So let us embrace the uncertain trail,
Together we rise, together we sail.
Through shifting ground, our spirits align,
In this journey, your hand in mine.

Portraits of Lost Wanderers

They roam the paths of fading dreams,
With hearts heavy like autumn leaves.
Silent whispers call their names,
In shadows where the lost believe.

Each step echoes with a sigh,
Footprints washed by the morning dew.
Their faces etched in twilight skies,
In colors lost, once vibrant hue.

Searching for a guiding star,
In the maze of time and space.
With every scar, they wander far,
Seeking solace, a warm embrace.

The voices linger in the air,
Fragments of laughter, tales untold.
In a world too bright, they fade to gray,
The lost wanderers, brave and bold.

Yet in their eyes, a flicker glows,
A spark of hope in the blind night.
Through fields of sorrow, beauty grows,
In portraits lost, they find their light.

The Ebb and Flow of Existence

Life rolls like waves upon the shore,
A dance of highs and lows in play.
Moments rise, then fall once more,
In the tides that shape our day.

Each heartbeat holds a secret song,
A rhythm woven through the years.
In the quiet, we find we belong,
Yet in the noise, we shed our tears.

Memories drift like ships at sea,
Some anchor deep, others float away.
Through storms of doubt, we long to be,
In the calm before another fray.

With every dawn, we start anew,
Each sunset marks what we let go.
In the cycle, we find what's true,
In the ebb and flow, our spirits grow.

Life's fleeting moments softly call,
Invite us to embrace the now.
For in this dance, we rise and fall,
Caught in existence, we take a bow.

Chasing Shadows of Yesterday

In the twilight of memory's glow,
Footsteps echo through the past.
Chasing shadows, moving slow,
Each moment a ghost, too fleeting to last.

Faded photographs in the mind,
Whispers of laughter woven with tears.
What we lost, we seek to find,
As time reveals our hidden fears.

Through the corridors of regret,
We wander, lost in the silent plea.
Shadows of yesterday linger yet,
Haunting the corners of what could be.

Yet in the dusk, we find a light,
A flicker of hope amidst the gray.
For even shadows, in their flight,
Can lead us to a brighter day.

So we chase, though the path be dark,
With hearts ablaze, we rise anew.
In every step, we leave our mark,
Chasing shadows, seeking what's true.

Bridges Built from Ashes

From the remnants of a shattered dream,
We gather hopes like scattered dust.
With weary hands, we start to seam,
Bridges from ashes, from ashes we trust.

Each broken piece tells a story,
Of battles fought, of love and loss.
In the scars, we find our glory,
Constructing paths across the cross.

Though flames have swept the past away,
In the embers, we see a spark.
With courage found in disarray,
We step boldly into the dark.

These bridges rise from what once was,
A testament to strength and will.
Through trials faced, we find our cause,
To build anew, our dreams fulfill.

In unity, we forge ahead,
With every step, our spirits soar.
From ashes, let our lives be fed,
Bridges built, forevermore.

Reflections in a Broken Mirror

Shattered pieces on the floor,
Dreams disperse like fragile glass.
What once was whole, now feels sore,
Truths in fragments, shadows pass.

Faces change in every shard,
Memories flicker, dance, and fade.
Life's paths often seem so hard,
Yet beauty in the pain is made.

A glimpse of self, both near and far,
Each fracture tells a tale anew.
The journey leads, a guiding star,
In brokenness, we find what's true.

Lessons learned in splintered time,
Reflections bend but seldom break.
We rise again, and still we climb,
In every scar, a chance we take.

Through jagged edges, light will gleam,
In unity, we find our song.
Embrace the chaos, chase the dream,
In shattered mirrors, we belong.

The Journey into Our New Skin

A metamorphosis unfolds,
Changing shapes beneath the light.
Discovery in stories told,
From cocoon's shade to flight's delight.

Transcending limits, shedding fears,
Each layer lost, a new is born.
In silence, heartbeats pulse and cheer,
Emerging strong, no longer worn.

Bruised by time, yet bold anew,
Each scar a mark of battles won.
We search for selves, for what is true,
In the embrace of the rising sun.

The journey's long, but paths align,
With every step, we forge ahead.
In every breath, the world is fine,
In new skin, we learn, we're led.

Embrace the change, the joy, the pain,
For in this dance, we truly live.
In all our rhythms, there's no gain,
Without the love we choose to give.

From Seeds to Giants

In the earth, a promise waits,
Tiny whispers in the ground.
From humble origins, fate creates,
A place where strength and growth abound.

Sprouting dreams through dark and cold,
Each tender sprig, a tale begins.
Nature teaches the brave and bold,
In every loss, a chance to win.

Roots entwined, they seek the sky,
Reaching high for sunlit grace.
Through storms and trials, they defy,
For giants stand, they find their place.

With every ring, they thrive and swell,
Wise with age, they learn to bend.
In silent strength, their secrets tell,
Of journeyed pathways without end.

From seeds to giants, time will show,
The power held within small starts.
In life's vast garden, love will grow,
Uniting all our beating hearts.

The Thread of Evolution

A thread runs through the fabric made,
Connecting all in endless weave.
From simple forms to life displayed,
In every strand, we learn, believe.

With each mutation, shifts arise,
Nature pens her endless prose.
From ocean depths to mountain highs,
A tapestry of life that flows.

Adapt and change, the constant dance,
In shadows cast by ancient light.
Every creature takes a chance,
To find its path, embrace its plight.

Fossils whisper, secrets shared,
In timeless tales of what has been.
In every being, love declared,
Evolution's song, a joyful din.

Threads entwined in symphony,
A melody of life's great quest.
In unity, we find the key,
To understand we are all blessed.

Unraveling in Harmony

Soft whispers float on the breeze,
A dance of shadows in the trees.
Each note a thread, entwined with care,
Connected hearts, a love we share.

Harmony swells, a gentle refrain,
Echoing joy, soothing the pain.
Together we walk through the light,
With every step, our spirits ignite.

In the silence, the world can speak,
A melody found in moments unique.
In colors that blend, we find our way,
A tapestry woven, forever to stay.

From the chaos, beauty emerges,
Like rivers that flow, each emotion surges.
We dance in the warmth of the sun,
In harmony's grip, we are one.

So let us unravel, a journey grand,
With every heartbeat, hand in hand.
Together we rise, let our spirits soar,
Unraveling in harmony, forevermore.

Shattered Pieces

In the silence, whispers of pain,
A heart once whole now bears a stain.
Shattered pieces on the floor,
Fragments of love, lost evermore.

Each slice of glass reflects the light,
Reminders of dreams that took flight.
Through the cracks, new visions gleam,
In each scar, an echo of a dream.

In the ruins, hope starts to grow,
A fragile bloom in the afterglow.
Every tear tells a story true,
Of battles fought, and courage renewed.

Time blends the scars, mends the soul,
From the ashes, we become whole.
With each dawn, the sun will rise,
Shattered pieces, transformed in the skies.

So gather the shards, embrace the pain,
For in the cracks, wisdom remains.
With every piece, a lesson learned,
In shattered glass, new light returns.

New Beginnings

The dawn breaks softly, a gentle light,
A canvas waiting, pure and bright.
With every step, we shed the past,
Embracing dreams, our hearts hold fast.

In the silence of morning's glow,
Hope whispers softly, 'Let go.'
With courage found in the unknown,
New beginnings are seeds we've sown.

The winds of change carry our fears,
But in their breath, the future nears.
Each moment a chance, a fresh restart,
New beginnings awaken the heart.

With open arms, we welcome grace,
Journeying forth at our own pace.
In every heartbeat, life sings true,
New paths await, just for me and you.

So let us leap, with spirits free,
Into the horizon, just you and me.
For in this journey, we're never alone,
New beginnings lead us to our own.

The Symphony of Our Colors

Brushstrokes vibrant, a canvas wide,
Each hue a story, deep inside.
Together we blend, creating art,
The symphony of colors, a beating heart.

Crimson whispers of love's embrace,
Azure echoes of a tranquil space.
Golden laughter dances in the air,
Every shade a moment we share.

In the chaos, beauty finds form,
Woven through storms, we stay warm.
Together we paint our world anew,
With every color, a promise true.

So let us celebrate this vivid theme,
A masterpiece forged from every dream.
In the gallery of life, we play our part,
The symphony of colors, a work of heart.

In every note, in every hue,
A testament of what we pursue.
Together we rise, together we sing,
In the symphony of life, together we bring.

Serpents of Old

In shadows deep, the serpents lie,
Whispers of darkness, echoing sighs.
Twisted tales of times gone by,
Lessons learned where legends die.

With scales that shimmer, they weave their fate,
Guarding secrets behind the gate.
Echoes of wisdom flow through their veins,
In the silence, knowledge remains.

They dance through the night, elusive and sly,
Slipping between the earth and sky.
In their presence, we confront our fears,
The past speaks gently, it draws us near.

In every coil, a story unfolds,
Sacred and ancient, the serpent holds.
Through cycles of time, they show the way,
From darkness to light, night to day.

So heed the lessons of serpents old,
In their gazes, wisdom told.
For in their dance, we find our role,
Embracing the shadows, they make us whole.

Wings of New

On the breeze, soft whispers play,
With wings of new, we find our way.
Breaking free from the chains of yore,
With every beat, we yearn for more.

In vibrant skies, our spirits soar,
Chasing dreams just beyond the shore.
With courage stitched in every seam,
We brave the winds of a new daydream.

In the dance of life, we take our flight,
With colors bright, we chase the light.
Each flutter a step, each turn a chance,
In the journey of hearts, we begin to dance.

So spread your wings, let go of fear,
Embrace the world that draws us near.
For in the skies, our souls align,
With wings of new, we shall always shine.

With every sunrise, a promise made,
In the path of hope, our worries fade.
Together we fly, through skies so blue,
With the wings of new, we start anew.

Among the Remnants We Carry

Among the remnants scattered wide,
Memories linger, never to hide.
Pieces of moments, fragments of light,
In shadows we tread, both day and night.

Whispers of laughter, echoes of cries,
Nestled within where our heart lies.
Each step we take, a story to tell,
Among the remnants, we weave our spell.

Time paints the canvas, colors so bold,
In every tale, some warmth, some cold.
Cherished and burdened, they shape who we are,
Among the remnants, we reach for a star.

Through trials faced, we rise anew,
Building our strength from all we've been through.
Among the remnants, seeds take flight,
In the darkest of hours, they seek the light.

Together we carry these pieces so dear,
Embracing the past while shedding the fear.
Among the remnants, we find our grace,
In the arms of time, we find our place.

The Unseen Growth

Beneath the surface, roots entwine,
Silent whispers, nature's design.
In stillness, secrets begin to bloom,
The unseen growth, dispelling the gloom.

From cracks in the soil, new life breaks free,
A testament of hope for the wise and the free.
Each gentle rise, a story to share,
The unseen growth, a dance of care.

Through seasons' change, we learn and adapt,
In moments of silence, the heart's been mapped.
The unseen growth, a journey profound,
In the quiet of life, new paths are found.

Soft petals open, revealing their hue,
In the darkest of nights, the dawn breaks anew.
Embrace the unfolding; let patience reign,
The unseen growth, our joy and our pain.

For in every struggle, there's beauty in sight,
The unseen growth, a beacon of light.
With tender embrace, like a nurturing hand,
We rise from the ashes, together we stand.

Fractured Dreams

In shattered fragments, hopes take flight,
Beneath the shadows of sorrow's night.
Each piece a story, a wish once bright,
Fractured dreams linger, searching for light.

We gather the shards with trembling hands,
A mosaic formed from life's demands.
Each aspiration taught us to grow,
Fractured dreams guiding us through woe.

When storms of doubt cloud the skies above,
We cling to the remnants of what we love.
With every tear, let's rewrite the scheme,
For within our hearts, we forge new dreams.

The tapestry woven with threads of despair,
A journey of healing, we learn to repair.
Fractured dreams turn to visions anew,
A promise of hope in the morning dew.

So let us embrace the beauty of breaks,
For through our struggles, the soul awakes.
Fractured dreams are not lost but revealed,
In the heart's quiet whisper, the truth is concealed.

Reclaimed

In quiet moments, we take back the night,
Reclaimed memories, shining so bright.
The echoes of laughter, the songs of the past,
In every heartbeat, true joy is cast.

With open arms, we embrace the whole,
Every lost fragment makes us more whole.
Reclaimed paths lead to wonders unseen,
In the dance of the cosmos, we reign with a dream.

The whispers of storms, the calm after rain,
In each gentle breath, we shatter the chain.
Reclaimed our spirits, a fierce, burning flame,
We rise from the ashes, unbound we reclaim.

With courage as armor, we break through the strife,
In the portrait of time, we flourish in life.
Every step forward, a tale to be told,
Reclaimed treasures, more precious than gold.

So let us journey, hand in hand, together,
In the tapestry woven, light as a feather.
Reclaimed our stories, a symphony grand,
In the dance of existence, forever we stand.

The Silent Symphony of Change

In the rustle of leaves, a whisper is heard,
The silent symphony sings each word.
With every moment, the world rearranges,
In subtlety born, life softly exchanges.

A dance of the seasons, a breath of the earth,
In the stillness of time, we measure our worth.
The silent symphony, a melody vast,
In the quietest echoes, we're freed from the past.

Through valleys and mountains, the river flows free,
In the pulse of the cosmos, we find harmony.
The silent symphony calls to the brave,
In the heart's gentle throb, a journey to save.

With each dawn rising, the canvas renews,
In the silence, we find the hues we choose.
The silent symphony, our spirits aligned,
In the whispers of change, love intertwined.

So listen closely, for change has a song,
In the quiet, we learn where we belong.
The silent symphony echoes throughout,
In our hearts, in our souls, it's a wondrous route.

Milton Keynes UK
Ingram Content Group UK Ltd.
UKHW021159251124
451300UK00024B/149

9 789916 791172